☩ur Catholic Life

A READING AND STUDY GUIDE FOR ADULT FAITH FORMATION

7

☩ PRAYER ☩

PRAYING OUR WAY THROUGH LIFE

Bill Huebsch

TWENTY-THIRD PUBLICATIONS

twentythirdpublications.com

IMPRIMATUR

+   Most Reverend Joseph R. Binzer
    Auxiliary Bishop
    Archdiocese of Cincinnati
    February 9, 2016

The *Imprimatur* ("Permission to
Publish") is a declaration that a
book or pamphlet is considered
to be free of doctrinal or moral
error. It is not implied that those
who have granted the *Imprimatur*
agree with the contents, opinions,
or statements expressed.

TWENTY-THIRD PUBLICATIONS
1 Montauk Avenue, Suite 200, New London, CT 06320
(860) 437-3012 » (800) 321-0411 » www.twentythirdpublications.com

ISBN: 978-1-62785-169-5
Library of Congress Catalog Card Number: 2016939657
Printed in the U.S.A.

Contents

How to use this study guide in seven small-group sessions

Gather. As people arrive for each session, welcome them warmly and offer them refreshments. You may wish to have sacred music playing to set the tone. If people are new to each other, name tags can help break the ice. When everyone has arrived, gather your group and invite them to open their books to today's material.

Begin with *Lectio divina* prayer. Each session opens with a short and prayerful reflection on a scriptural text that is found in that section of the *Catechism*. Here are the steps:

1. Begin with the Sign of the Cross.

2. Read aloud the Introduction for this session.

3. Call everyone to prayer using these or similar words: *Let us turn our hearts to Christ now and hear the word of the Lord.*

4. Invite a member of the group to proclaim the Scripture we present for you.

5. Invite your group members to share about the text, first in twos and threes if you wish, and then as a whole group. Sharing: *What word or phrase in this reading catches your ear? What is God saying to us in this scriptural text?*

6. Now pray in these or similar words:
    O God, we know that you are with us and that you behold all we are about to do. Now grant that, by the power of the Holy Spirit, we might be faithful as we study our faith and charitable in how we treat each other. Through Christ, our Lord. Amen.

Read. Moving around the circle in your group and rotating readers, read aloud each numbered faith statement. Group members should note items in the material that strike them as especially important. Do not read aloud the **We Believe** statements. They are provided as an enhancement to the text.

Group or personal process. When you come to the process notes, pause to continue around the circle, discussing as the notes direct. Use our suggestions as a starting point, and add your own questions, prayers, or action plans.

Finish. As you conclude this session, call everyone to prayer once again. Reread the scriptural text we used in the beginning. Then move around the circle one last time to share: *In light of this reading and what we have learned today, what has touched you most deeply? What new insight of faith will you carry away from here? What new questions about faith have arisen for you? How will today's discussion work its way into your daily life?* Close your session with the prayer we provide, or lead a spontaneous prayer in which everyone shares their own prayer.

Session One

BASED ON ARTICLES 1066–1109 AND 1113–1130 OF THE
CATECHISM OF THE CATHOLIC CHURCH. **TO READ A SUMMARY OF THIS**
SECTION, SEE *CATECHISM* **ARTICLES 1110–1112 AND 1131–1134**

Introduction

We turn now to study the way Catholics pray. We will consider both the public prayer (known as the liturgy) of the Church as well as the more personal and private prayer lives we hope to cultivate. We'll wind up this study by an in-depth look at the Lord's Prayer.

First, the Church's liturgy. In the liturgy of the Church, God the Father is blessed as the source of all the blessings of creation with which he has blessed us in Christ, in order to give us the Spirit as sons and daughters of God. Christ's work in the liturgy is sacramental because his body, which is the Church, is like a sacrament (sign and instrument) in which the Holy Spirit dispenses the mystery of salvation and because through her liturgical actions the pilgrim Church already participates, as by a foretaste, in the heavenly liturgy. The mission of the Holy Spirit in the liturgy of the Church is to prepare the assembly to encounter Christ. The sacraments are signs of grace, instituted by Christ and entrusted to the Church, by which divine life is shared with us. The visible rites by which the sacraments are celebrated signify and make present the graces proper to each sacrament.

Scripture

READER: A reading from the Letter to the Ephesians.

For this reason I bow my knees before the Father, from whom every family in heaven and on earth takes its name. I pray that, according to the riches of his glory, he may grant that you may be strengthened in your inner being with power through his Spirit, and that Christ may dwell in your hearts through faith, as you are being rooted and grounded in love. I pray that you may have the power to comprehend, with all the saints, what is the breadth and length and height and depth, and to know the love of Christ that surpasses knowledge, so that you may be filled with all the fullness of God. (EPHESIANS 3:14–19)

READER: The word of the Lord.

ALL: Thanks be to God.

PART ONE + ARTICLES 1066–1083 OF THE *CATECHISM*

Why the liturgy?

[1] God is love that desires to be shared. In Christ, that love is revealed to us; it is incarnated; it is love in the flesh. And in the Spirit of love "we live and move and have our being." In this way, love is shared by us all in a huge, generous, and free gift that comes directly from the heart of God!

[2] Down through the centuries, God prepared us through words and deeds to be evermore ready to receive this gift: the revelation of God. In Christ, that work was completed, and for that reason we celebrate above all the paschal mystery when we celebrate liturgy.

[3] The *Constitution on the Sacred Liturgy* from Vatican II emphasizes this in article 2: "The divine sacrifice of the Eucharist," it says, "is supremely effective in enabling the faithful to express in their lives, and portray to others, the mystery of Christ and the real nature of the true Church."

[4] The word "liturgy" comes to us from two Greek words, one meaning "work," and the other meaning "for the people." For us Christians, it refers to our participation in God's work, the work of God in the world. It is a reference to worship, yes, but also to living as the body of Christ, proclaiming the Good News and living in charity.

WE BELIEVE

In the liturgy of the Church, God the Father is adored as the source of life and blessing; this blessing is given to us through his Son, Jesus Christ, and we are adopted as sons and daughters through the power of the Spirit.

---

[5] And as the Constitution says, there is no other work and nothing else we Christians do that is more powerfully effective in achieving this! Because of this, liturgy shapes our identity and forms our lives as Christians. For this reason, Vatican II called forcefully for the full, conscious, and active participation of all!

[6] The beautiful Letter to the Ephesians expresses this sense of prayer when the writer, speaking on behalf of the whole Church, prays in chapter 3, verses 16 and 17: "May [God] grant that you be strengthened in your inner being with power through [the Holy] Spirit, and that Christ may dwell in your hearts through faith, as you are being rooted and grounded in love."

[7] Being "rooted in love" is the work of liturgy and, of course, the first desire of God for us. The liturgy, therefore, is the source of our lives, and also the goal. In practical terms, this means that our daily lives each week are directed to our eventual gathering as church in liturgy, and our whole week also flows from that liturgy as water from a fountain! Because of this, it is linked directly to all we do, especially to catechesis.

Mystery and celebration

[8] Let us return to that lovely letter to Ephesus to which we referred earlier here, to chapter 1, verses 3 through 6. "Blessed be the God and Father of our Lord Jesus Christ, who has blessed us in Christ with every spiritual blessing..."

[9] Blessing is a divine and life-giving action. Its source is always God, and it leads us to know and love God in return. All of divine work is one vast blessing for us, for we ourselves have been blessed, first with a covenant of love, and then with constant grace to live in love, especially in those astonishing events: the birth of Isaac to Sarah in her old age, the escape from Egypt, the gift of the promised land, the election of David, the presence of God in the Temple, the purifying exile, and the return of a "small remnant."

[10] In the liturgy, we return God's wonderful blessings and offer ourselves in love, offering the very gifts we have received and, thereby, blessing the whole world.

Group or personal process

*   What are the blessings of your life? How do you bring those to Mass with you? To your daily prayer?

*   How do you bless others?

It is Christ who acts

[11] In liturgical celebration, it is Christ who acts by communicating God to us. The sacraments are visible, tangible, audible words and actions or signs that make God present.

[12] In a mysterious way, Christ's own dying and rising, which we call the paschal mystery, is not an event swallowed up in the past like all other historical events. It is still present every time we celebrate the liturgy. The event of the cross and resurrection remains with us and draws everything toward life.

[13] In other words, Christ is always present in liturgy: first in the people gathered, and in a distinct way, in the priest who serves as presider for the celebration, and also in the sacred words and deeds, especially in the Eucharist.

[14] It is Christ who baptizes, Christ who forgives, and Christ who heals and makes us whole. It is Christ who is present in the word broken open and shared. Alleluia!

The work of the Spirit

[15] As for us, it is the Spirit of love, the Holy Spirit, who prepares our hearts to receive Christ in sacraments and celebrations. The history of liturgical prayer is as old as the People of God ourselves. Throughout the history of this common prayer, the Spirit has been our guide, and when we pray now as Christians, we include elements of ancient prayer as well as those of the newer covenant.

[16] For example, we read from the Old Testament, pray the Psalms, and remember the stories of our ancestors. Now those ancient

events and people have new meaning for us because, by the light of our Christian faith, we see them also in a new light.

[17] Because of this important connection, we reread these stories often during certain seasons: Advent, Lent, and the Easter Vigil. When we assemble now in the name of Christ, bringing our ancient faith and stories with us, we do so in the power of the Spirit of love who gathers us into one, transcending all human categories such as race, culture, and social standing.

[18] Sunday is the "Lord's Day" for us Catholics, a day set aside for liturgy and rest. We should always be well prepared for Sunday Mass, allowing our hearts to be near to God and opening ourselves to the grace we receive. How does this preparation unfold? Always through the power of the Spirit.

[19] The Spirit comes to us in the word of God, as we break it open and share it. The Holy Spirit gives a spiritual understanding of this word to those who read or hear it, according to the readiness of their hearts. The Holy Spirit also helps us *remember,* and to remember is very important to us. Remember what?

[20] Nothing less than the powerful actions of Christ, the dying and rising, the washing of our feet, the service of his life, and the gift of his Body and Blood. We give a name to this act of remembering: "anamnesis." Anamnesis is remembering the wonderful expressions of God that we have seen.

[21] Not only do we remember these things, but they are actually made present once again each time we celebrate the liturgy. These events are not repeated, then, but celebrated in the Spirit of love. When we pray together at liturgy, we call upon God's Holy Spirit, the Spirit of love, to be with us and bless what we do. We give a name

to this act of petition: "epiclesis." Epiclesis is calling on God who is present already to bless us and our gifts.

[22] It isn't that we think the Spirit is absent. Rather, we humans must do this; we must call on God to bless us, lest we ever forget… So, whenever we gather for liturgy, it is the Spirit who unites us into a communion. We become what we celebrate then: the body of Christ.

WE BELIEVE

The mission of the Holy Spirit in liturgy is to prepare the hearts of the faithful so that we might encounter Christ. The Spirit makes the saving work of Christ present in each liturgical celebration.

---

[23] The most intimate cooperation of the Holy Spirit and the Church is achieved in the liturgy. And the Spirit also makes the liturgy effective within us and within our daily lives. We become a living offering to God, God's own people, united in work for the reign of love.

Group or personal process

- What do you want the Spirit to bless in your life?

- Write your own prayers of anamnesis and epiclesis to use as a table prayer in your home. Each time you pray at table, you enter into both forms of prayer.

- What does it mean that the paschal mystery is central in our understanding of liturgy, as we learned in faith statements #19–21 above?

Our theology of sacrament

[24] Everything we do in liturgy in the Church is centered on the Eucharist and the sacraments. We celebrate seven sacraments, and they all share certain common points in their theology or doctrine.

In Christ

[25] All of our sacraments were instituted by Christ, that is, they emerge from his own life and ministry. In a sense, you could say, the sacraments continue now in our own time and place the work he did. They empower us, each in its own way, for ever greater love and service within the body of Christ.

In the Church

[26] Over the centuries, the Church has gradually recognized that Christ has given us a treasure through his own life and ministry, and we now believe there are seven expressions of that ministry that hold pride of place among the others. We are what we pray and celebrate, so the sacraments, in a sense, "make the Church what it is in the world."

WE BELIEVE

The sacraments are visible, tangible, and audible signs of grace, instituted by Christ and entrusted to the Church. The rites make present the graces proper to each sacrament.

[27] We are the body of Christ as Church, so when Christ acts, we act too in sacramental celebrations. The faithful celebrate the liturgy

with the ordained, who are appointed to a special role. The role of the ordained is to serve the rest, guaranteeing that it is really Christ who acts whenever we celebrate.

[28] Through the ordained, we are connected to the apostles, and that connects us to Christ in an important way. When one is baptized and confirmed, and when one receives holy orders, he undergoes a deep, interior change because the Spirit touches his heart to call him, open him, and empower him for worship and service.

In faith

[29] When Jesus sent his apostles to go and make disciples, he was sending them to announce Good News, namely, that God has established a reign of love open now to all people. Implied in this is the mission to baptize as well, since through baptism people begin the journey of faith.

[30] After all, the purpose of the sacraments is to help make us holy, and the chief way to holiness is love. There is an old saying that we believe according to how we pray. And it's true: our liturgical celebrations form us in faith, perhaps more than any other single act.

[31] We humans need certain set patterns of worship that we call "rites," and we maintain them carefully, changing them only as a whole Church, only rarely, and only under the guidance of the Spirit.

For salvation

[32] When we speak of salvation, we refer to the process of being made whole, of being empowered for love in a radical way by the life and death and resurrection of Christ. The sacraments play a vital role in this because through them we receive grace, and grace is God communicating God's own very self to us. And in God's love

we grow able to love ourselves, rejecting selfishness, acting less uni-laterally, and living in the Spirit.

[33] The sacraments are powerful because in them, Christ acts re-gardless of how worthy we are. Christ acts with power. Christ acts with love. Nevertheless, the fruits of the sacraments also depend on the disposition of the one who receives them.

[34] For those of us called to Christ, the sacraments are necessary for salvation, according to article 1129 of the *Catechism*. The sac-raments give us a share in the divine life by uniting us with Christ.

For eternal life
[35] If we live in love, we will die in love, and we will live in love eternally. The sacraments are a sure way for us to do this, and they give us a "blessed hope" that we will always live in peace.

Group or personal process

- The sacramental life of the Church is such a rich and powerful part of who we are as Catholics. What has your participation in the sacramental life of the Church meant to you? How has it helped you to develop your relationship with God and with others?

- As you think about your experience of the sacraments, what memories stand out for you? What moments of sacramental celebration—Mass, reconciliation, matrimony, or others—linger in your memory as unique moments of encounter with Christ and the community?

- How have the sacraments shaped you as a Catholic?

Prayer

O God, grant that we may be strengthened in our inner being with power through the Holy Spirit. May the Spirit well up within us like a fountain of fresh water. May Christ dwell in our hearts through faith. May the grace of mercy and forgiveness, of kindness and love, fill our actions, words, and thoughts. And may we be rooted and grounded in your love as we leave this gathering to return to our everyday lives. We pray through Christ, our Lord. Amen.

Session Two

THE PEOPLE, PLACES, AND RITES OF THE LITURGY

BASED ON ARTICLES 1135–11186 AND 1200–1206 OF THE
CATECHISM OF THE CATHOLIC CHURCH. TO READ A SUMMARY OF THIS
SECTION, SEE CATECHISM ARTICLES 1187–1199 AND 1207–1209

Introduction

Having been reintroduced to the theology of liturgy in the last lesson, let us turn now to understanding *how we Catholics celebrate*. The Liturgy of the Word is an integral part of each liturgy celebrated by the Church. It is important to us because Scripture is so important to us. We will learn again that Sunday is the principal day for the celebration of the Eucharist because it is the day of the resurrection. It is the preeminent day of the liturgical assembly, the day of the Christian family, and the day of joy and rest from work. Sunday is "the foundation and kernel of the whole liturgical year." And we will learn that the Church, "in the course of the year... unfolds the whole mystery of Christ from his Incarnation and Nativity through his Ascension, to Pentecost and the expectation of the blessed hope of the coming of the Lord." And before we end, we will learn as well that the diverse liturgical traditions or rites, legitimately recognized, manifest the catholicity of the Church, because they signify and communicate the same mystery of Christ.

Scripture

READER: A reading from the First Letter of Peter.

But you are a chosen race, a royal priesthood, a holy nation, God's own people, in order that you may proclaim the mighty acts of him who called you out of darkness into his marvelous light.

Once you were not a people, but now you are God's people; once you had not received mercy, but now you have received mercy. (1 PETER 2:9–10)

READER: The word of the Lord.

ALL: Thanks be to God.

PART ONE + ARTICLES 1135–1152 OF THE CATECHISM
We all celebrate liturgy!

[1] We begin here with the *Constitution on the Sacred Liturgy* that was enacted at Vatican II. In that great document that now shapes the Church itself, we read that liturgical prayer is not private because it is always a celebration of the Church.

[2] It is the whole body of Christ who prays each time any of us does, but it is also true that individual members play varying roles, are touched in varying ways, and pray in varying cultures. It is for this reason that the Constitution says, in article 27, that "rites which are meant to be celebrated in common, with the faithful present and actively participating, should, as far as possible, be celebrated in that way rather than by an individual..."

[3] It goes on to say that this is especially true of the Mass and all of the sacraments. The Constitution also states: "It is very much the wish of the Church that all the faithful should be led to take that full, conscious and active part in liturgical celebrations which is demanded by the very nature of the liturgy...to which the Christian people," it says, quoting now from the First Letter of Peter, "'a chosen race, a royal priesthood, a holy nation, a redeemed people' have a right and to which they are bound by reason of their baptism."

WE BELIEVE

The liturgy is the work of the whole Church. Each member of the assembly has a role to play, and all are called to full, active, and conscious participation. The ordained preside in their role of bringing "holy order" to the community.

---

[4] Powerful words, these, and the basis really of all the reforms enacted by Vatican II. How we pray is who we believe ourselves to be. If the whole Church prays at liturgy, then the whole Church sees itself as church.

[5] But not all members of the Church play the same role in the celebrations themselves. There is a role, for example, for the ordained, who represent Christ among us, "standing in" as it were as Christ's vicar. And there are roles for others who may not be ordained: lectors, musicians, servers, extraordinary ministers of communion, and others.

Signs and symbols

[6] The signs and symbols we use in liturgy emerge from nature around us as well as from our culture. In daily life, signs and symbols are very important. We express love with them, and we express the inexpressible using language, gestures, objects, and actions. God "speaks to us" in the same way, using the most common elements of daily life: water, bread, wine, oil, a touch, or a word.

[7] God also speaks through actions, and sometimes actions speak louder than words: washing, anointing, breaking bread, sharing a common cup, or tracing on our bodies the sign of the cross. Once these signs and symbols are used by us to express our faith, they are no longer common; they become holy. This has always been true for the human family.

[8] Christ himself used signs and symbols freely, and we take our lead from him. Now these signs are imbued with the power of the Holy Spirit, the Spirit of love, and they signify much more than they are!

Group or personal process

- How do you "speak" with actions, gestures, objects, and words to express the inexpressible in your own life?

- What signs and symbols of the liturgy are most important to your spirituality? How do they contribute to your prayer, meditation, and spiritual growth?

- What is your role in the liturgy? What various roles have you played over the course of your lifetime?

Meeting God

[9] In sacramental celebrations, like the Mass or any of the sacraments, we humans meet God the Creator, we experience Christ, and we are given the Spirit to live in our hearts forever. Through our actions and words, something inexpressible is finally said: Repent and believe. The kingdom is at hand.

[10] The Liturgy of the Word is integral to our sacramental celebrations, and every sacrament has this element. The signs with which this word is proclaimed should be clear and evident: the book of the word itself, how we venerate that word when we proclaim it, audible and understandable reading, the homily and the response of the faithful.

[11] Music is an essential part of liturgy as well, combining sacred music and words to inspire and uplift our hearts. Music can really move us! It should, therefore, be beautiful, should allow for all to sing together, and should be solemn and prayerful. Because it is so important to us and because it touches us so deeply, the words of the music must be carefully chosen to accurately reflect our faith, be drawn from Scripture, and be completely singable!

[12] Likewise, the use of sacred images and art should be of restraint and beauty rather than sumptuous display. Sacred art, such as statues, paintings, and sculpture, helps us express the same gospel message that Scripture communicates by words. Image and word illuminate each other. Every work of art or sacred image should lead us to see Christ, who is God incarnate. Even images of Mary or the saints should always lead us to Christ.

The liturgical year

[13] The Church observes a cycle of feasts and seasons, repeated annually, through which we remember the mysteries of our faith. Since the time of Moses, and maybe before him, the People of God have followed such a calendar.

[14] In the Christian calendar of feasts, each Sunday is special. It is a celebration of the resurrection of Christ, and the memorial of God's "rest" in Genesis during the creation of the world. On this day, we celebrate the Lord's Supper in our assembly, and this eucharistic supper is the central activity of our shared life. Even though we also celebrate Mass each day, the celebration on Sunday holds pride of place because this is when the whole Church assembles.

WE BELIEVE

The Church unfolds the whole mystery of Christ beginning in Advent, moving to his teachings and works, to his Passion and death and resurrection, to Pentecost, where the Spirit empowers the Church to continue to unfold the work of Christ in the world.

----

[15] During Holy Week we celebrate three days that commemorate Christ's passion and death as well as his glorious resurrection. We give a name to these three days: "Triduum," a word that means, literally, "three days." We mention this first in considering the liturgical year because it is central to all the rest of the year. These are the "high holy days" of the Christian calendar.

[16] The liturgical year begins with the First Sunday of Advent, continues through Christmas to Epiphany, opens up a short period of Ordinary Time before Ash Wednesday, and then launches headlong into Lent, culminating in Triduum and Easter. After

Easter there is a period called "the fifty days" which is that period leading up to Pentecost, exactly fifty days after Easter each year. And after Pentecost, we shift back into Ordinary Time again until the First Sunday of Advent rolls around and we start all over again!

[17] Ordinary Time refers to the largest period of the year except Advent–Christmas and Lent–Easter. It is called "ordinary" not because other times are somehow more "extraordinary" but because it pertains to everyday life, to the normal flow of time...We also keep a secondary calendar during each liturgical year, on which we commemorate feasts of Mary and the saints. We honor Mary especially, and the saints as well, because they lead us to Christ.

[18] Within each day we also celebrate certain moments of prayer in a form that allows our whole day to be wrapped up in praise of God. We call this prayer by a name: "Liturgy of the Hours." We used to call it the "Divine Office." The Church urges all members, religious, lay, or ordained, to pray this daily, especially morning praise, midday prayer, evening prayer or vespers, and nighttime prayer or compline. The Church provides an approved form for this prayer. The Liturgy of the Hours is rooted in Scripture.

Group or personal process

- In the course of the liturgical year, which feast and holy days speak most loudly to you?

- How is Sunday an important day to you, and how do you make it a special day?

- Make a chart showing the principal high points of your own personal year. Include things like birthdays, anniversaries, memorials, civic holidays, and Church holy days. This is your personal "liturgical calendar."

- How does the Triduum touch your heart? How does it strengthen your call to die to yourself as you imitate Christ? How does the promise of resurrection affect you?

- Tell a story of a time when you practiced the art of self-giving love, when you gave up yourself or part of your money, time, or property, when you carried a cross for someone, and when you experienced the joy of rising in Christ afterward.

PART THREE + ARTICLES 1179–1186 AND 1200–1206 OF THE *CATECHISM*

Where do we celebrate?

[19] To be honest, *where* we celebrate our liturgies is not as important as that we do so faithfully. The churches we build, in nations where we are allowed to, are not merely gathering places but also a sign of God's people. But these buildings are not the Church itself. We, the People of God, *are the Church*.

[20] And yet...We must have a gathering place, and the churches we build for this purpose should be in good taste and designed for liturgy. The altar should be dignified and as humble as the Lord's cross. The tabernacle should be in a place of honor, and it should be secure.

[21] The holy oils that are used in anointing at baptism and confirmation, anointing of the sick and holy orders, should likewise be in a place of honor. The chair should be placed so that the presider can be seen directing the prayer. The lectern or ambo should give

dignity to the word of God and be placed so that the attention of the faithful can easily be directed to it. Each church must have a suitable baptismal font, as well as holy water fonts to foster among the faithful a remembrance of their baptismal promises.

[22] The renewal of the baptismal life requires penance. A church, then, must have suitable rooms designed for celebrating the sacrament of reconciliation. And the church must be a space that invites quiet prayer, recollection, and common prayer. The church is a place for all God's people, and therefore, it should be open and welcoming.

Liturgical rites

[23] Even though the liturgy we pray around the world is one and the same, it is always set in a cultural context with diverse forms of ritual. The mystery of Christ is so unfathomably rich, the *Catechism* tells us in article 1201, that it cannot be exhausted by its expression in any single liturgical tradition. Our various rites and traditions complement one another and make the Church rich.

WE BELIEVE

It is fitting that liturgy expresses itself in the culture of the people who are present. The Church is universal, and her liturgy matches that worldwide presence. This manifests the Church as truly "catholic."

[24] These liturgical traditions have developed because the Church is universal and made up of many different peoples. Each of the various traditions expresses the faith of the culture and people who celebrate it. In this way, Christ reaches out to all people, while maintaining unity in love and charity.

[25] Here is a list of some of the traditions presently in use in the

Church: Armenian; Byzantine; Coptic; East and West Syrian; Ethiopian; Latin, often called "Roman"; and Maronite. The *Constitution on the Sacred Liturgy* tells us in article 4 that the Church recognizes all these rites and holds that they are "of equal right and dignity" and that the Church wishes "to preserve them in the future and to foster them in every way."

Liturgy and culture

[26] The liturgy should correspond to the genius and culture of all the different peoples of the world. It should be celebrated in ways such that these cultures are not abolished by that, but fulfilled. We journey together to God, each as we are called.

[27] Certain parts of the liturgy cannot be adapted and must be common to all: the use of water in baptism, the bread and wine in Eucharist, the oil in confirmation, the words of reconciliation, the bond of matrimony, the laying on of hands in ordination, and the anointing with oil for healing, among others.

Group or personal process

- What do you look for in a church building? What makes it really "a church" for you? How do you distinguish between the building and the People of God who are the living Church?

- How do you make the place where you live into a domestic church? What signs, symbols, or actions do you have there? What household rituals do you observe that are holy and sacred to you and your household?

- How has your parish included the cultural expressions of the people in its worship, structures, events, or ministries?

Prayer

*O God, you have made us a chosen race and a people
of your own. You have also made us into a royal priesthood;
each of us has a calling and role to play in building up the reign
of God. And you have made us into a holy nation; you have formed
us as a people. We are, indeed, a redeemed people by reason of our
baptism. We now turn our hearts to you once again, and we open
ourselves to whatever you call us to do and become. May our royal,
priestly, and chosen place as your sons and daughters be transformed
into discipleship. We pray through Christ, our Lord. Amen.*

Session Three

BASED ON ARTICLES 2558–2589 OF THE *CATECHISM OF THE CATHOLIC CHURCH*. TO READ A SUMMARY OF THIS SECTION, SEE *CATECHISM* ARTICLES 2590–2597

Introduction

We shift our attention now from formal liturgical prayer to personal time spent with God. In prayer, the Holy Spirit raises our mind and heart to God. We will learn that prayer is a privileged moment of intimacy with God where we discuss our lives, the needs of the world, and the ways our heart moves within us. We allow God to thank us for our work, to have a laugh together, to remind us of our sinfulness and selfishness, and to rest in the comfort of each other's presence. God calls each person to this mysterious encounter with Godself. Thus, prayer unfolds throughout the whole history of salvation as a relationship between God and us.

Scripture

READER: A reading from Psalm 130.

Out of the depths I cry to you, O LORD. Lord, hear my voice! Let your ears be attentive to the voice of my supplications! If you, O LORD, should mark iniquities, Lord, who could stand? But there is forgiveness with you, so that you may be revered.

(PSALM 130:1–4)

READER: The word of the Lord.

ALL: Thanks be to God.

PART ONE + **ARTICLES 2558–2567 OF THE CATECHISM**

A surge of the heart

[1] St. Thérèse of Lisieux, also called the Little Flower, wrote a profound and joyous book encouraging an attitude of unlimited hope in God's merciful love. "For me," she wrote, "prayer is a surge of the heart; it is a simple look turned toward heaven, it is a cry of recognition and of love, embracing both trial and joy."

[2] In prayer, the Holy Spirit works in us, raising our mind and heart to God, requesting good things from God, and offering God our own selves. We have within us an inborn hunger for God, we seek to drink of the divine well, and Christ stands ready to give us a drink.

[3] Early in John's gospel is a story that reveals this mystery. Jesus is speaking with a woman near a well. He asks her for a drink and they begin a wonderful conversation. In it, Jesus teaches her that everyone who drinks from the well by which they stood would become thirsty again. "But those who drink of the water that I will give," he told her, "will never be thirsty." For the water Jesus promised would become an inner wellspring, "gushing up to eternal life!"

[4] This is the wellspring of prayer, with Jesus as its source, and eternal life as the outcome. For us Christians, prayer is the response of faith to the free promise of salvation and also a response of love to the thirst of the only Son of God. When we pray, it is always our

entire self in prayer, but it is our heart that swells and heals. When our heart is near to God, when we cultivate this closeness, prayer flows like water from that well.

[5] And when our hearts are far from God, our words of prayer are in vain. By this we don't mean our biological hearts, but the center of our persons, that place where we are most true. The heart is where we make a covenant with God, the place where the divine indwelling becomes an encounter that sustains us.

[6] In prayer we move toward God, and God moves toward us. It is a twofold relationship, a joint effort, with the Spirit of love guiding us on every step.

[7] In prayer, we encounter the Triune God aside from all our theology and rational thinking. In prayer, we come to know God as Father, or perhaps as Mother. It is the father of the prodigal child waiting and watching, hoping we will come home. It is the mother of the sick child in Tyre and Sidon, trusting in and demanding—even arguing for—Jesus' healing touch.

[8] In prayer, we come to know Christ as the revelation of God who is love. It is the discovery of the reign of God among us, and the joy of dying and rising in Christ. In prayer we come to know the Spirit as the energy of love and a powerhouse of grace.

All are called

[9] Down through history, we humans have sought God. We are in search of God still. Even though we bear that dark inclination to selfishness, to unilateral choices, yet there remains that inner voice calling us home to God. In prayer, we are always responding to God's call. God's initiative comes first and we enter into a mysterious, divine encounter.

Group or personal process

- When is it most difficult for you to pray?

- When you pray, how do you address God? What kind of things do you pray about?

- How do you hear God calling you to spend time talking with him in the intimate encounter that is prayer?

PART TWO + ARTICLES 2568–2584 OF THE *CATECHISM*

Down through history

[10] Prayer is the glue that binds human history, for history tells of the unfolding relationship between God and us. The first nine chapters of the Book of Genesis are filled with figurative language about God communicating with us humans.

[11] We are said to have offered God thanksgiving gifts, to have walked with God in the evening, to have called on the divine name, to have been blessed by God for upright living, and to have received God's promise of fidelity. But the most dramatic encounter

with God, for the entire human family, is told through the story of Abraham and Sarah.

[12] Abraham was attentive in his heart to the will and desire of God for him. What is it that drew Abraham and Sarah forth to leave the land and people they knew and venture into the unknown, following their hearts? Abraham's prayer is made in silence, as he welcomes that mysterious guest to pause on his journey and join him for a meal, as told in Genesis, chapter 18, verses 1–15. Abraham kept his heart attuned to the divine voice echoing in its depths.

WE BELIEVE

The encounter between Moses and God helps us understand that God wants to walk with us. God wants us to respond to his law, which is written upon our hearts. The prayer of Moses foreshadows that of Jesus Christ.

---

[13] Likewise Jacob, who wrestled with a mysterious figure much as we might wrestle with a mysterious idea or question or problem. Jacob persevered that night; and so must we.

[14] The voice of God continued to echo down through the years. Using figurative language once again, Scripture depicts God speaking from a burning bush. Moses, balking and questioning at first, listened well in the end and followed where that voice led him. This is a call to leadership, to difficult work as a servant of the people. Moses remained attentive to the divine voice, from Egypt through the desert to Sinai.

[15] There is a wonderful line in the desert story told in Exodus, chapter 33, verse 11. "Thus the Lord used to speak to Moses face to

face," it says there, "as a man speaks to his friend." Moses had become a contemplative, speaking with God often, at length, face to face and heart to heart. Buried deep in this divine-human relationship is trust, and sometimes bold and dramatic demands.

[16] When the people had built their golden calf and given up on the God Moses knew so well, God threatened to let his wrath burn hot against them. But Moses refused to accept the divine wrath and implored God to reconsider. He reminded God of the divine promises, of the marvelous deeds, and of the people who had held fast with great faith. "And the LORD changed his mind," Exodus tell us.

[17] And then there was David, psalmist, leader, and king. He is the shepherd who prays for the people, the one chosen among Jesse's sons, a willing-if-not-always-faithful servant, and a loving and joyful songster. David's prayers would be the model for Jesus and for all of us even today.

[18] The prophets were those who spoke for God, calling the people to be faithful, to live with justice for the poor, and to turn their hearts to God. Elijah is perhaps the prophet whose voice echoes to our own day most loudly. After God had taught Elijah mercy in a wild place called Wadi Cherith, Elijah become more attentive to the voice of God in his depths. He finally took the desert road that led to the place where God reveals the divine self, to Mount Horeb. This story is told in 1 Kings, chapter 19. There Elijah listened for God's voice but it was not found in the great wind, or in an earthquake that followed, or in the fire...Indeed, Elijah, standing at the entrance of his cave, heard the voice of God in "the sound of sheer silence."

[19] Each of us is called to this same mysterious encounter with God, speaking in our own depths. Each of us is called to pray always. Like the prophets who drew light and strength from prayer,

our prayer will help us face the challenges and opportunities of this world head-on. We learn from the prophets, as from Abraham and Moses and David, to be attentive to the divine voice and to respond in faith.

Group or personal process

- How does God speak to us in prayer?

- What can we learn from our ancestors in the faith about the voice of God?

- Read faith statement #15 again. What resonates in this for you? Do you talk with God as you would with a friend? Do you laugh? Do you hear God thanking you for your work and love?

PART THREE + ARTICLES 2585–2589 OF THE *CATECHISM*

The Psalms

[20] The great book of prayers in the Old Testament is the Book of Psalms. Not all the psalms were written by King David, and in fact this collection has many authors. These were liturgical hymns used mainly in Temple worship. In Hebrew they are called "Tehillim," which means "praises." In Greek, the name is "Psalmoi," which means religious songs set to music. There are 150 Psalms.

[21] We Christians pray the Psalms as our own, sharing them with our Jewish sisters and brothers and all men and women of good will. They arose from the hearts of those people liv-

ing in the Holy Land and outside it, but they speak in a voice that echoes for all. The Psalms both express and celebrate God's saving works.

I believe in music

[22] In the world of the Hebrew people living during the time of King David, singing was a chief way people expressed themselves. There were no *recordings* of music, of course, until very recently, so if there was to be music, it had to be sung.

[23] Sometimes people sang happy songs, sometimes the songs were sad. Sometimes the songs expressed tremendous gratitude for what God had done. Sometimes they expressed tremendous anger at what God had *not* done! And sometimes they just sang about the wisdom of living as children of God. The psalms cover all these aspects of the human heart.

WE BELIEVE

The Psalms are a master class on prayer.
They are both deeply personal and strongly communal.
They extend to every dimension of life, and they
express our human dependence on God.

---

[24] Nobody's happy all the time. Sometimes you just feel down in the dumps. And sometimes you feel like you're really ready to "sing the blues." Some of the psalms also do just that. They're called "songs of lament." The lament psalm is the most common type. Almost one-third of all the psalms are sad like this. Some are the kind of lament a whole community shares, like when you're being persecuted as a group. And others are more private laments, like when

you have a personal misfortune, such as when you get sick or when misfortune strikes your household.

[25] Sometimes it's possible to think that God has forgotten you. The crops are dry but no rain comes. People mock you for your faithfulness. Your most important relationships are lost. You lose heart. The lament psalms express this kind of feeling, but they almost always move to express trust and thanksgiving, sometimes before God has even had time to answer their prayer! Here's a sample of some lament psalms: Psalm 12 begs for help in these evil times. Psalm 35 is a long prayer for deliverance from one's enemies. Psalm 60 is a communal prayer for victory. There are about 40 lament psalms in the Book of Psalms.

[26] Other psalms express simple praise and prayer to God, resting in God as in a mother's bosom. This provides a powerful counterpoint to the often masculine images of God that appear in traditional renderings. The people praised God by singing the "praise psalms." They believed that God was the cause of all that is good.

[27] And they believed that God gave them victory over their foes. This made them happy, so they sang about it. Many of these psalms end with a blessing. Here's a list of some of the psalms of praise: Psalm 8 sings of God's greatness! Psalm 19 describes the glory of God in the heavens. Psalms 145–150 are a group of psalms that all sing God's praise.

[28] There are a whole group of psalms that help us live as God's children. These are wonderful "wisdom psalms" that express confidence in God's wisdom over ours. One can pray these psalms or parts of them every day. Here's a list of some of the wisdom psalms: Psalm 1 speaks of two ways one might travel through life. Psalm 32 describes the happiness of those whose sins are forgiven. Psalm 37

is a long exhortation to live in wisdom.

Group or personal process

- Have you ever felt so bad that you began to think maybe God had abandoned you? Tell what that was like? How did you move beyond that moment in your life?

- Read back through faith statements #23–28. Which of the psalm styles suits you best at this moment in your life? Why?

- Write a psalm for yourself, using one of the forms of the psalms discussed here.

Prayer

(Share your personal psalms with each other or pray using these or similar words.)

Jesus, you send the Spirit to create within us a spirit of prayer. May we experience that surge of the heart; may we learn to take a simple look inward, a cry of recognition and of love, embracing both trial and joy. And may your words to that woman at the well, promising that those who drink of the water that you give will never be thirsty again, fill our ears with joy. And may we, like Moses, experience prayer with you "face to face, as [one] speaks to his friend." We pray for this grace of prayer, in your holy name. Amen.

Session Four

**BASED ON ARTICLES 2598–2619 AND 2623–2643 OF THE
CATECHISM OF THE CATHOLIC CHURCH. TO READ A SUMMARY OF THIS
SECTION, SEE *CATECHISM* ARTICLES 2620–2622 AND 2644–2649**

Introduction

Let us now turn our attention to the various forms of prayer that we
Catholics have known down through the centuries. We will learn
that the Holy Spirit who teaches the Church and helps us remember all that Jesus said also instructs us in the life of prayer. The basic
forms of prayer are blessing, petition, intercession, thanksgiving,
and praise. And we will learn that the gospels provide an image of
Jesus as constantly prayerful. In the final analysis, our study here will
reveal that, because God blesses the human heart, it can in return
bless God, who is the source of every blessing.

Scripture

READER: A reading from the Letter of Paul to the Romans.

Likewise the Spirit helps us in our weakness; for we do not know
how to pray as we ought, but that very Spirit intercedes with sighs
too deep for words. And God, who searches the heart, knows what
is the mind of the Spirit, because the Spirit intercedes for the saints
according to the will of God. (**ROMANS 8:26–27**)

READER: The word of the Lord.

ALL: Thanks be to God.

PART ONE ✝ ARTICLES 2598–2606 OF THE *CATECHISM*
The Word

[1] When God chose to speak to us humans in our own time and in our own language, God did not speak many "words" but only a single, powerful Word. That Word, Jesus Christ, reveals prayer to us in a dramatic and stunning way. If we first contemplate Jesus in prayer, as the gospels present it to us, and then listen as Jesus teaches us, we will know how to pray as well.

Jesus in prayer

[2] Like us, Jesus learned to pray as he grew. Perhaps the first lesson may have come from his parents, Joseph and Mary. When you pray with Mary, as the Gospel of Luke tells it, you hear a prayer of the heart. "My spirit rejoices in God, my Savior," she prays. And Joseph, we assume, prayed with attention to that divine voice sounding in his heart; for Joseph, God's voice led him, guided him, and became a trusted source of inspiration.

[3] And Jesus also learned to pray from his fellow Jews, picking up the rhythms and seasons, the psalms, prophets, and poets.

[4] But there is another source for Jesus, another teacher, and it rests deep in his own heart. There, in the same mysterious encounter that Abraham and Sarah had experienced, that Moses had known,

that had inspired David, and that had driven the prophets, Jesus encountered God.

[5] The Gospel according to St. Luke is a school on prayer. In it, the author portrays Jesus as a man of prayer and offers up for us tremendous lessons. Prayer is what leads Jesus; being attentive to the divine voice echoing in his heart, Jesus trusted in what he heard. And so must we be attentive and trusting.

[6] At Jesus' baptism, before he heard God's voice, before calling the disciples, before expanding his public ministry, before asking his disciples that intimate question, "Who do people say I am?" before God's voice sounded on the mountain, before teaching his own followers how to pray, before breaking bread at supper, before accepting his cross, before forgiving his killers, before surrendering his spirit for the final time—before any of these moments, Jesus prayed.

WE BELIEVE
Jesus' prayer as God's Son is the model for all the praying we do.
Often done in solitude and secret, Jesus' prayer shows a loving relationship with his Father, one in which he had absolute confidence that whatever God asked of him—even the cross—would lead to goodness.

---

[7] These ten great moments of prayer in Luke's gospel show how attentive Jesus was to God's voice and how deeply attuned he was to the divine source of love. The gospel writer has laid out for us a pattern of prayer that we can adopt.

[8] The other gospels likewise present Jesus as a person of prayer. In a sense, Jesus' entire proclamation of the reign of God is set in the

context of "attentiveness." "Pay attention!" he might have said, "and you will learn the mysteries, the secrets of God's kingdom."

[9] Taken together, the gospels reveal an understanding that is the foundation of prayer for us. When we pray with gratitude and confidence, God speaks to us in return, but God does not speak many words.

[10] The word that God speaks to us in prayer is Christ himself, the Word of God. And when we receive that Word, we ourselves become "other Christs"; we become the word to others; we become the word to the world.

[11] In the Gospel of John, Jesus blends a farewell speech to his followers with a profound prayer to his Father. Beginning in chapter 14, we find comfort, consolation, and peace in Jesus' words. "Do not let your hearts be troubled...I am the way...I will do whatever you ask in my name...I will not leave you orphaned...I am the true vine... Love one another as I have loved you...Ask and you will receive... Father, the hour has come...Father...I made your name known to them..." Amen.

Group or personal process

- When have you heard the voice of God in prayer calling you to become another "Christ" for someone or in some situation?

- Prayer opens us up to whatever God is asking us to do. How has God led you to be merciful, kind, loving, or generous in ways that you may not have expected?

The prayer of faith

[12] As we have just seen, Jesus taught us to pray by praying himself. And God's response to Jesus' prayer was Jesus' own very life, that life as oriented toward God and focused on God's orientation to him.

[13] His pathway to God is one we can also follow. We learn to pray by listening to Jesus, the teacher. The first step in prayer is conversion, the turning of the heart toward Christ, orienting ourselves toward God.

[14] Part of conversion is always reconciling with others who are our sisters and brothers in Christ, being at one with the community of Christ which is the Church. This leads us to love our enemies, to forgive seventy times seven times, to hold no grudge and withhold no favor, to pray in secret, to be attentive to God's voice, and to keep our hearts pure and open so that the divine voice can resound there.

[15] Above all, conversion leads us to seek the kingdom of God and to give up our lives for it. We orient ourselves toward God, in other words, when we orient ourselves toward God's people.

[16] Conversion is ongoing throughout our lives, not once-and-for-all and forgotten. As it takes hold of us and our hearts are attuned to the divine voice echoing within us, we learn to pray in faith. And this is the second step: listening to God in prayer.

[17] Jesus assures us that we can and should ask, seek, and knock on the figurative divine door. God will answer indeed. When we orient ourselves toward God, God will indeed be oriented toward us.

[18] And how much faith should we bring to prayer? Reflecting our long tradition of faith, the Gospel of Mark suggests to us that we can trust entirely in prayer. "Whatever you ask for in prayer," Jesus teaches in chapter 11, verse 24, "believe that you have received it, and it will be yours."

[19] Remember the faith of the Roman centurion in the story told in Matthew, chapter 8, or of the Canaanite woman in chapter 15. These came to Jesus believing, and they went away receiving. In contrast, Jesus' own disciples seemed not to believe. "Why are you afraid, you of little faith?" he asked them once.

WE BELIEVE

Mary's prayer in saying yes to God and in her wonderful song, the Magnificat, shows the generous offering of her whole being to God. We are also called to respond the same way.

---

[20] The prayer of faith requires us to make ready our own hearts. There are three parables in the gospels that help us grasp what this means. The first, in Luke, chapter 11, is the story of the friend coming at night; it invites us to urgent, trusting prayer. "Ask, and it will be given you."

[21] The second, in Luke, chapter 18, is the story of the widow and the judge, and it is centered on how to pray without ceasing; with the patience of faith we keep our hearts attuned to God. The third parable is also in Luke, chapter 18, and it is the story of the tax collector; this story helps us understand the role of humility in one who prays. "God, be merciful to me, a sinner!" the tax collector says. If our hearts are ready and steadfast, if our hearts are open and strong, God, we are assured, is already responding!

[22] The prayer of faith is powerful. Jesus often assured those around him that their faith had made them well, their faith had brought them peace, or their faith was their prayer. We learn about the prayer of faith from Mary. Her prayer was her very life, lived in tune with God's powerful grace. She offered her whole being to God as we must also do, saying, in essence, "Here I am." This is Christian prayer: to be wholly God's, because God is wholly ours.

Group or personal process

• How do you develop the idea of "praying always"? The idea of having your own heart in a constant state of readiness to hear God's voice in its depths?

• Do you believe that God responds to us when we pray? What form does that response take?

• How is Mary a model of faithful prayer for you? What other women have you known in your life who had her trust and courage in prayer?

PART THREE + ARTICLES 2623–2643 OF THE *CATECHISM*
Forms of prayer

[23] From the earliest years of Christian history, we have believed that it is the Spirit who prompts us to pray. The second chapter of Acts of the Apostles paints a picture of life in the early community: teaching and fellowship, breaking of bread, and the prayers.

[24] We have traditionally named five forms of prayer, although certainly others exist as well. These forms flow from our liturgical traditions and are rooted in Scripture, especially in the Psalms and prayers of Christ.

Blessing and adoration

[25] Blessing describes the basic encounter between God and us humans. God blesses us and we bless God. Our blessing prayers are directed to God in the power of the Spirit through Christ. God's blessing returns to us in like manner. Adoration is a mental posture in prayer, a way of standing before God with our hands and hearts open to God's wonder. It is a sense of awe in light of all that God does: in creation, within us, and in sharing love so endlessly with us.

Petition

[26] When we turn to God and beg for mercy, or for health for a sick child, or for good weather for our crops, or for any other need, we ask, not because God is unaware, but because by asking, we turn our hearts to the divine source. We must be converted anew each and every day; we must turn our hearts to Christ over and over again.

WE BELIEVE

Praying to become forgiving, praying to seek the kingdom of God, and praying for God's blessing are true petitions.

---

[27] St. Paul reminds us of this in his Letter to the Romans in chapter 8, a beautiful chapter that is all about life in the Spirit. Toward the end of the chapter, in verse 26, he reminds us that the Spirit helps us "for we do not know how to pray as we ought." Indeed, all prayer originates in the marriage of our own self with the Spirit of love. And

of course, the first sentiment and prayer is to ask forgiveness. Asking forgiveness is the prerequisite for both the eucharistic liturgy and personal prayer, which is why we open the Mass with a penitential act.

Intercession

[28] If petition is asking for our own needs, then intercession is asking on behalf of others. It is an ancient form of prayer in the Christian Church, and Jesus himself prayed on our behalf throughout his ministry and then sent the Spirit as our helper. When our hearts are attentive to God's mercy and to the voice of God echoing in our depths, intercession comes naturally to us as an act of charity and as the means by which charity increases.

[29] We are even encouraged to pray for our enemies, to bless and not to curse them. Prayer of intercession should lead to acts of intercession on behalf of the poor, the needy, the imprisoned, the injured, the outcast, and the rejected. Prayer "pushes" us to work for justice; in the words of the *Catechism* (2632), prayer leads to "collaboration with the mission of Christ and the Holy Spirit."

Thanksgiving

[30] Thanksgiving is the central prayer of the Church, shaped and formed as we are by the Eucharist. And why not? All we have and all we are has its origin in God.

Praise

[31] Praise is perhaps the one form of prayer that belongs most to our hearts. We become attentive to the urging and stirring of our hearts as we contemplate the wonders of God. That urging, that deep movement of Spirit and love that causes our hearts to swell with gratitude, to trust that our petitions are heard, and to be deeply committed to the needs of others, leads us to bless God for all we

have. And that swelling, that movement within us, is praise.

[32] Anyone can praise God with their lips, but to live a lifestyle of divine praises leads to holiness. Hence, praise embraces the other forms of prayer and carries them forward. We compose hymns and canticles of praise and we sing doxologies of praise, but finally it is our hearts that lead the way.

Group or personal process

- List the forms of prayer that we just learned about. Which of these forms—and there may be more than one—most speaks to you in your life right now?

- Share among yourselves how you have learned to turn your heart to Christ in prayer.

Prayer

Jesus, you promised that whatever we ask for in prayer will be ours if we but believe. Take away our lack of belief. Strengthen our hearts to believe. We are sometimes of so little faith and so much fear. May we become like Mary: powerful in grace. Like her, may we offer our whole being to you and say, in essence, "Here I am." We belong to you and our prayer leads us home to your presence. May we become wholly God's, because God is wholly ours. We pray in your holy name. Amen.

Session Five

THE WELLSPRINGS OF PRAYER

BASED ON ARTICLES 2650–2660, 2663–2679, AND
2683–2691 OF THE *CATECHISM OF THE CATHOLIC CHURCH.*
TO READ A SUMMARY OF THIS SECTION, SEE *CATECHISM*
ARTICLES 2661–2662, 2680–2682, AND 2692–2696

Introduction

We must now consider how prayer arises in our souls and leads us to the heart of God. The Holy Spirit in the Church, we will learn, is the one who teaches us to pray as the children of God. Furthermore, we will learn that it is the word of God, the liturgy of the Church, and the virtues of faith, hope, and charity that are sources of prayer. Knowing this, we will then turn our attention to the different schools of Christian spirituality and learn how they share in the living tradition of prayer; these will become for us precious guides for the spiritual life. Finally, we will learn that it is the Christian family that is the first place for education in prayer.

Scripture

READER: A reading from the Gospel of Matthew.

"All things have been handed over to me by my Father; and no one knows the Son except the Father, and no one knows the Father except the Son and anyone to whom the Son chooses to reveal him. Come to me, all you that are weary and are carrying heavy burdens, and I will give you rest. Take my yoke upon you, and learn from me; for I am gentle and humble in heart, and you will find rest for your

souls. For my yoke is easy, and my burden is light."
(MATTHEW 11:27–30)

READER: The word of the Lord.

ALL: Thanks be to God.

PART ONE + ARTICLES 2650–2660 OF THE CATECHISM
The will to pray

[1] Prayer is, in part, a decision on our part to set aside the time, to find the proper place, to use the needed tools, and to learn how to pray. The believing and praying Church can help open us to the flow of the Holy Spirit who is our teacher. This "living transmission" is called Tradition, and down through the centuries the Church has passed from generation to generation the secrets of prayer.

[2] In the heart of the person who prays, the Spirit becomes like a fountain of water—fresh, excellent, living water. In the Christian life there are several sources or "wellsprings" of prayer.

The word of God
[3] The first wellspring is the Scripture itself. The pastors of the Church encourage all Catholics to go to the sacred Scripture often, to study it and learn how to read it, and, above all, to pray with it. It isn't enough simply to become educated about the texts without also allowing them to touch you. It isn't so much a process of study as of "breaking open" these texts in the light of the Holy Spirit. This leads to meditation and contemplation, the greatest gifts of prayer.

The liturgy of the Church

[4] Sometimes we attend liturgy so frequently and know so well its rhythms and prayers that we sit through the Mass without praying. It takes effort on our part—intentional effort—to enter into liturgy with a prayerful heart and to think back to it afterward with gratitude and praise.

The theological virtues

[5] We enter into prayer, of course, with the eyes and ears of *faith*. But we also enter into prayer with *hope*. Hope is nourished within us as we pray, especially when we pray the psalms and prayers of Scripture. St. Paul seemed to understand this when he wrote these lines in the Letter to the Romans, chapter 15, verse 13: "May the God of hope fill you with all joy and peace in believing, so that you may abound in hope by the power of the Holy Spirit."

WE BELIEVE

The word of God, the liturgy, and the virtues of faith, hope, and charity are the sources of prayer. The Spirit teaches us to pray.

[6] Of course, the way to holiness and peace, in fact the way to everything God promises, is *love*. Prayer draws everything into love and love is the real source of prayer. Perhaps no one has captured this more acutely than St. John Vianney, the Curé of Ars, in *Prayer*. "I love you, O my God, and my only desire is to love you until the last breath of my life. I love you, O my infinitely lovable God, and I would rather die loving you, than live without loving you. I love you, Lord, and the only grace I ask is to love you eternally..."

"Today"

[7] St. Paul urged the Christians of his day to pray always. And while it's true that we pray at liturgy or in the appointed hour of the day, a heart that is attentive to God is always at prayer. Such prayer allows us to see the events and news of each and every day through the lens of faith.

[8] It is today that we encounter Christ, not yesterday and not tomorrow. Prayer happens today. But such ongoing prayer must be learned. We learn to have sacred pauses in each day, moments when we let go of the activity, turn down the volume, and tune into our own hearts. What do we hear there? What do we sense? What word is God speaking within us?

Group or personal process

• Which of these "wellsprings of prayer" is more effective for you? What other wellsprings do you experience?

• What is your experience of hope as you pray? How does hope grow within you during prayer?

• Does your prayer lead you to acts of charity? Give some examples.

• How do you keep yourself attentive during liturgy, opening your heart to what God seeks to reveal to you in the readings, prayers, community, and shared Eucharist?

The way of prayer

[9] The way of prayer for the Christian is always through Christ. Regardless the time or place or method of prayer, we enter into the divine presence with Christ as our teacher and source of grace.

[10] When we pray through Christ, we use a variety of invocations: Son of God, Word of God, Lord and Savior, Lamb of God, Good Shepherd, our Life, our Light, our Hope, or simply, Friend. But the one name that sums it all up, the name that is above all others, the name given at his birth, is Jesus.

[11] In this name, the divine and human flow together and all faith and love merge. In writing to the Christian community in Philippi, St. Paul urged them to know Jesus. "Let the same mind be in you that was in Christ Jesus," he wrote in chapter 2, verses 5–11, "who, through he was in the form of God, did not regard equality with God as something to be exploited. Rather, he emptied himself, taking the form of a slave, being born in human likeness...every tongue should confess that Jesus Christ is Lord."

[12] Perhaps the simplest prayer is one that we can memorize: "Come, Lord Jesus. Come." Calling on the name of Jesus is the simplest way of praying always. When his name is repeated often by a humbly attentive heart, spiritual blessings flow into our lives.

[13] But, of course, as St. Paul reminds us, "No one can say 'Jesus is Lord' except by the Holy Spirit." The pastors of the Church urge us to live in the Spirit and to dwell with the Holy Spirit daily. The simplest and most direct prayer is also

a very traditional one: "Come, Holy Spirit, fill the hearts of your faithful, and enkindle in them the fire of your love."

WE BELIEVE

Prayer is primarily directed to God as Father, but also toward Jesus and the Spirit. We also love to pray in communion with Mary, who always leads us to God.

---

[14] The Holy Spirit, whose presence fills our whole being, is the interior teacher of Christian prayer. To be sure, there are as many ways to pray as there are persons who pray, but it is the same Spirit acting in all.

[15] It is always true that we pray to God through Christ our Lord in the power of the Holy Spirit. It is also true that Mary, his mother and ours, shows us the way of fidelity and prayer and is herself a sign of that way of prayer. From the annunciation of Jesus' conception to the foot of the cross, Mary followed the way of prayer.

[16] When we pray with Mary, we remain centered on Christ as she did. And like her, our prayer blesses God for the many good things we have. We also entrust to Mary our needs. She is our mother, the one who holds our hopes in her own heart. We have a simple and traditional prayer, one that arises from the texts of Scripture.

[17] "Greetings, favored one! The Lord is with you," the angel said to Mary. "Blessed are you among women, and blessed is the fruit of your womb," Elizabeth her cousin said when they met at the door. The traditional formula for this prayer echoes these scriptural passages: *Hail Mary! Full of grace. The Lord is with you. Blessed are you among women and blessed is the fruit of your womb, Jesus!*

[18] Medieval piety in the Latin rite in the West developed the prayer of the Rosary as a popular substitute for the Liturgy of the Hours. In the East, the litany called the Akathistos and the Paraclesis remained closer to the choral office in the Byzantine churches. The Armenian, Coptic, and Syriac traditions preferred popular hymns and songs to the Mother of God.

Group or personal process

- What are the memorized prayers, or the frequent short prayers, that are dear to your own heart?

- At this point in your life, what is your prayer relationship with the Blessed Virgin Mary like? How has it changed over the years?

- Besides Mary, what other members of the communion of saints do you call on in prayer?

PART THREE + **ARTICLES 2683–2691 OF THE** *CATECHISM*
Guides to prayer

[19] We do not learn to pray alone nor do we ever approach God without one another. That is the beauty and power of the Church.

[20] Every time we pray, for example, we pray with all those who have gone before us, marked with the sign of faith. Their prayer remains powerful, and their divine contemplation is our hope.

[21] The first place we learn to pray is our home, the household of faith where we live in a "domestic church." Teaching young children to pray daily and praying with them at home is the most powerful formation in prayer. Prayer cannot be taught like arithmetic or reading; it must be learned by apprenticeship, by example, and by spiritual osmosis.

[22] The household of faith is where this occurs by having sacred objects within sight, a family Bible that is read and treasured, sharing meals as often as possible, welcoming guests with affection, seeing the events of the world through the lens of faith, being part of a parish community, and allowing everyday activities to demonstrate God's presence.

WE BELIEVE

The Christian family and household is
the first place where children learn to pray.

---

[23] Pastors in the Church also play a vital role in helping form members of the Church in prayer. By their example and exhortation they lead people to seek Christ, to pray the liturgies, and to celebrate life's turning points. Many religious have consecrated their whole lives to prayer. From the early years of the Church until now, hermits, monks, and nuns have devoted their time to praising God and interceding for his people.

[24] Parish catechesis programs aimed at children, youth, and adults also have a role to play in forming us in prayer. Such catechesis for the whole community makes use of liturgical prayer in a special way, making it the source and summit of life. It encourages and teaches personal prayer, meditating on the Scriptures, reading the lives of

the saints, or memorizing certain key prayers that we carry with us always.

[25] Prayer groups can become "schools of prayer" for many people today. They should be encouraged and assisted to pray as the Church prays.

[26] Some of the faithful have the gift of discernment, a gift of the Holy Spirit, to serve as spiritual directors for others. This is a high calling and great responsibility, for whatever spiritual life the director leads, his or her disciples will also.

Where to pray

[27] Choosing where we will pray can be very important to our success. Certainly the local parish church building is the proper place for the Sunday assembly. In fact, most liturgical celebrations will be observed in the parish church, but some, such as anointing of the sick, may not.

[28] It might also be fitting from time to time for us to make pilgrimage to local shrines or to monasteries where we are welcome. Or it may be fitting to pray before the Blessed Sacrament in the quiet light of the parish church. Or perhaps to make a retreat for more intense prayer.

[29] For personal prayer, we might develop a sacred space within our home somewhere, or perhaps the sacred space we need is on a walk through nature or along the sea coast. We should not think that sacred art and icons are meant only for churches or that they are a thing of the Church's past. Having such a space within our household encourages and models prayer for all.

Group or personal process

- Where do you pray best? What is that space like?

- Think back over the past week. Consider the week day by day. Recall the moments when prayer occurred for you, or when it may have been possible but did not occur. How would you grade yourself?

- Who taught you to pray? How did they do that?

Prayer

O God, may you be our source of hope and fill us with all joy and peace in believing so that we may abound in hope by the power of the Holy Spirit. May we pray with St. John Vianney, the Curé of Ars: "I love you, O my God, and my only desire is to love you until the last breath of my life. I love you, O my infinitely lovable God, and I would rather die loving you, than live without loving you. I love you, Lord, and the only grace I ask is to love you eternally..." We pray through Christ, our Lord. Amen.

Session Six

WAYS TO PRAY AND OBSTACLES TO PRAYER

....

BASED ON ARTICLES 2697–2719 AND 2725–2751 OF THE
CATECHISM OF THE CATHOLIC CHURCH. TO READ A SUMMARY OF THIS
SECTION, SEE *CATECHISM* ARTICLES 2720–2724 AND 2752–2758

Introduction

Sometimes we know that prayer is not easy. We must learn how to pray, and we must also confront the obstacles to prayer as they arise in our lives. In this lesson we will learn that the Church invites the faithful to regular prayer: daily prayers, the Liturgy of the Hours, Sunday Eucharist, and the feasts of the liturgical year. These regular prayers help us by providing a cadence of prayer in our lives. We will also learn that the Christian tradition comprises three major expressions of the life of prayer: vocal prayer, meditation, and contemplative prayer. They have in common the recollection of the heart. And we will consider the principal difficulties in the practice of prayer: distraction and dryness. Finally, we will learn that it is always possible to pray; it is even a vital necessity. Prayer and Christian life are inseparable.

Scripture

READER: A reading from the Gospel of John

"I ask not only on behalf of these, but also on behalf of those who will believe in me through their word, that they may all be one. As you, Father, are in me and I am in you, may they also be in us, so that the world may believe that you have sent me. The glory that you have given me I have given them, so that they may be one, as we are one, I in them and you in me, that they may become completely one, so that the world may know that you have sent me and have loved them even as you have loved me." (JOHN 17:20–23)

READER: The word of the Lord.

ALL: Thanks be to God.

PART ONE ✦ ARTICLES 2697–2719 OF THE *CATECHISM*

The life of prayer

[1] Sometimes we forget to pray at all; we forget to place ourselves in God's presence, and instead, we fill our lives with chatter and activity. In order to make prayer a habit of the heart, we must have specific times of prayer in each day.

[2] Traditionally these specific times of prayer have included morning and evening prayer, prayer before and after meals, the Liturgy of the Hours, and Sundays animated by the Eucharist, following the feasts of the liturgical cycle. Likewise, tradition has suggested three forms or major expressions of prayer: vocal, meditative, and contemplative. They have one basic thing in common: the readiness and vigilance of the heart.

Vocal prayer

[3] We often say or think words toward God, but our prayer is not so much the quantity, timing, or format of our words. It is the con-

dition of our hearts that matters in vocal prayer. Jesus taught us a wonderful vocal prayer known today as "The Our Father" or "The Lord's Prayer." He himself surely prayed aloud the liturgical prayers of the Jewish synagogue but also raised his voice at other key moments from joyous blessings to the agony in the garden.

[4] We are human beings with bodies, and we need our senses if we are to pray. In this way, with our hearts engaged, we pray with our whole being. Vocal prayer is often the common prayer of groups of Christians, but even private, internal prayer uses words.

WE BELIEVE
The Christian tradition has always had three expressions of the life of prayer: vocal, meditative, and contemplative. They all flow from the heart.

Meditation

[5] Meditative prayer is the prayer of searching, the mind seeking to understand, the heart seeking to be reconciled. It is difficult to sustain meditation for long, because our minds wander with busy-ness. Sacred books, sacred music, the Scriptures, icons, liturgical texts, spiritual writings, poetry, and even nature itself can all assist us in meditation.

[6] When we meditate on the mysteries of our faith, they become our own, mingled as they are with our very lives. If we are attentive, we sense that our hearts stir, and we experience enlightenment. There are many forms of meditation, and each person finds the one right for him or her. In meditation we think deeply, imagine the story unfolding around us, and employ our emotions and desires. But meditation's purpose is not to "figure things out" as much as to unite ourselves completely with Jesus.

Contemplative prayer

[7] Contemplative prayer is possible at any time, in any place, in any state of health, or in any phase of our lives. Nonetheless, it helps enormously for us to set aside time to pause and allow our hearts time to encounter the divine heart. In contemplative prayer, we gather up our lives, matters of the heart, daily routines, the news of the world, all gathered, all offered with grace to God.

[8] Contemplative prayer is nothing more than allowing God to dwell within us silently. There is a wonderful story told of St. John Vianney, the Curé of Ars. He noticed a fellow in his parish church, coming in a little way each day, sitting in a back pew, simply sitting. One day the Curé asked him, "What are you doing here, sitting silently each day?" The gentleman answered simply, "I gaze upon God. God gazes back at me." Contemplation.

[9] Contemplative prayer is the simplest expression of the mystery of prayer. It is a gift, a grace; if we choose to accept it, we do so in humility and gratitude. It is a focus on Jesus, a silent, loving moment between friends. In such prayer, the Word echoes loudly in life, even though we pray in silence. It renders us speechless, unable to find words.

[10] So we pause, setting aside time for Christ; we allow ourselves to be wrapped up in the moment, intense, silent, intimate, and loving. Slowly, little by little, we sense the movement of Spirit, the light in the darkness, the power of love. We are in communion with God who loves us so much! We are keeping watch with Christ.

Group or personal process

- Briefly define each of the expressions of prayer about which we have just learned.

- What are your experiences with each of these forms of prayer? Which come most naturally to you?

- Which form of prayer do you find most difficult?

- Why do we sometimes struggle to learn to pray, to enjoy time spent with God in prayer, and to be really honest and our most true selves with God?

PART TWO ✛ **ARTICLES 2725–2734 OF THE** *CATECHISM*

The struggle to pray

[11] We know that prayer is a gift, the work of the Spirit and grace, but it is also a response on our part, an intentional activity into which we enter. Sometimes, perhaps often for some of us, prayer is a battle, almost like a beam of light, fighting not to be overwhelmed by a room full of darkness.

[12] To be Christian is to pray and thus to be in communion with Christ. So prayer is essential for us, and difficult or not, we must undertake the work of prayer. In prayer, we are often our own worst enemy. We may, for example, have a poor view of prayer, thinking it's just some psychological activity, a purifying of the mind by our own effort.

[13] Or we may think we're supposed to empty our minds, resulting

in a mental void of some kind, to let prayer fill us up. Or for many of us, prayer is just ritual words and gestures, just going through the motions. So we fly through the Sign of the Cross, or mutter through the prayers at Mass, or recite our penance from reconciliation. For many of us, prayer is regarded as simply something we don't have time for, as if prayer were an activity incompatible with anything else.

[14] For some of us, only reason and science are valid, and prayer certainly is neither of those. Others of us prize being productive and achieving results and find that prayer interrupts our work. And some of us regard prayer as too "other worldly" to truly fit into modern life that is very "this worldly."

WE BELIEVE

In prayer, we must bring humility, trust, and perseverance to play. Despite temptations to think otherwise, prayer forms us in faith, and by it we are led to our true destiny and purpose.

---

[15] And for many, many of us, we have experienced what we would call "failure" in prayer. Our prayer life has become dry and lifeless, or we realize in prayer that we are called and we don't wish to follow the call. For example, to give what we have to the poor and then to follow Christ, like the rich young man in the gospels. Or we have come to believe that prayer is a sham, that God does not hear prayers because ours appear not to have been answered, or even, and perhaps this is the most insidious, we believe that there is no God at all.

Overcoming difficulties

[16] Sometimes in prayer, we feel distracted. We are there, finally, in prayer, but our mind is wandering from this to that, from one

anxiety to another. Our temptation is to work like mad to end this, when all we really need to do is simpler: turn back the heart with acceptance, and allow the meditation to resume. Allow each distraction to reveal to you that to which you are most attached: your children, money, work, sports…Simply shift this attachment to the Lord and all these others things will follow.

[17] Sometimes in prayer, we experience dryness. We are there, finally, in contemplation, but our heart feels empty and there is no light. We do not experience the warm glow and energy of love that we anticipate should be ours. Our temptation at these times is simply to quit, to give in to the dryness and seek some other source of refreshment. But all we really need to do is open our hearts, trust the intuitions that arise there, and follow God's initiative to love. This is a moment for sheer faith, believing against all odds.

[18] Sometimes in prayer the difficulty is lack of faith. We are there, finally, in prayer, but we are filled with many other concerns. We turn to the Lord only as a last resort, or we turn to Christ but presume that nothing will come of it. What we most need at these times is to pray for faith itself. We need to turn to Christ without petition, but only with gratitude, opening and developing our heart.

Group or personal process

- What are the greatest obstacles to prayer for you? How can you pray despite them?

- What distracts you from prayer the most?

- Do you really believe that prayer is useful or even possible? What evidence can you cite to support your belief?

Does God answer prayer?

[19] When we praise or thank God, we are not particularly concerned whether or not our prayer is acceptable. On the other hand, when we ask for something we want, we demand to see the results within minutes! What image of God is behind this? God is not a commodity or a vending machine but the Source of life and love.

[20] It is essential that when we pray we allow the Spirit to work within us and that we not dominate the prayer with our own needs. We do not go to prayer with our agendas all set and our demands ready. We go to prayer to see what it is that the Spirit wishes for us. Pay close attention to the deep mind, the heart, and the inner voice.

[21] Prayer makes us attentive to God speaking not many words or not with many unplanned interventions. No, in prayer God speaks a single profound word, and that word is nothing less than the life of the one who prays. We are the ones who are spoken. Our very lives, when they are oriented toward God and receptive of God's life, become God's word to the world.

Perseverance in prayer

[22] Love opens our hearts to three enlightening and life-giving facts about prayer. First, it is always possible to pray. It is possible and even beneficial to pray at the oddest times: while walking alone or with your friend, seated in a coffee shop, doing the laundry, mowing the lawn, or even cooking.

[23] Second, prayer is a vital necessity. Our hearts long for God and are not satisfied by anything less than communion with the divine. Third, prayer and the Christian life are one and the same, part and

parcel of each other. God is not absent from us, and Christ is not distant. Our prayer is not to God who is far away but to God who is among us, radically present and radically near at hand.

[24] Prayer introduces us to God, and that is all we really ever need. The author of the Gospel of John put it well in chapter 15, verses 16–17: "You did not choose me but I chose you. And I appointed you to go and bear fruit, fruit that will last, so that the Father will give you whatever you ask him in my name. I am giving you these commands so that you may love one another."

[25] In fact, the Gospel of John provides us with the longest single prayer that tradition places on the lips of Jesus. It fills all of chapter 17. We have traditionally referred to this as "the priestly prayer of Jesus," and rightly so. This is the prayer that was on the lips of Saint Pope John XXIII in calling Vatican II and inviting other Christians: "...that they may be one."

[26] This wonderful prayer brings together all of Jesus' work, especially the love that knows no end and the people who cling to Christ as their own. And lest we think that Christ has forgotten us, this prayer is our greatest source of hope: "I ask not only on behalf of these [here with me] but also on behalf of those who will believe in me through their word, that they may all be one." Indeed, may we all be of one heart and mind in Christ.

Group or personal process

- How does God answer your prayers? Do you ever feel that God fails you?

- How has prayer become a "vital necessity" in your life?

- On a day-to-day basis, how do you "stay in touch" with God, speaking with him about the events and opportunities for self-giving love that are embedded in everyday life? How do you enter into give-and-take with God?

Prayer

O God, we know that we did not choose you but that you chose us and you appointed us to go and bear fruit, fruit that will last. You promised that you will give us whatever we ask of you in the name of Jesus. This new command to pray leads us to love one another. Now we turn our hearts once again to you, O God. We know that you are near us, that you wait for us. We hear you calling us in the night and among your people. Increase our faith and trust in your word. We pray through Christ, our Lord. Amen.

Session Seven

THE LORD'S PRAYER

BASED ON ARTICLES 2759–2772, 2777–2796, AND 2803–2856 OF THE *CATECHISM OF THE CATHOLIC CHURCH*. TO READ A SUMMARY OF THIS SECTION, SEE *CATECHISM* ARTICLES 2773–2776, 2797–2802, AND 2857–2865

Introduction

No treatment of prayer would be complete without a long look at the Lord's Prayer. It is truly the summary of the whole gospel and the basic prayer of the Christian life. Praying to our Father should develop in us the will to become like God and foster in us a humble and trusting heart. In the Our Father, the object of the first three petitions is the glory of the Father: the sanctification of his name, the coming of the kingdom, and the fulfillment of his will. The four other petitions present our wants to him: they ask that our lives be nourished, healed of sin, and made victorious in the struggle of good over evil.

Scripture

READER: A reading from the Gospel of Matthew.

"When you are praying, do not heap up empty phrases as the Gentiles do; for they think that they will be heard because of their many words. Do not be like them, for your Father knows what you need before you ask him. Pray then in this way: Our Father in heaven, hallowed be your name. Your kingdom come. Your will be done, on earth as it is in heaven. Give us this day our daily bread. And forgive us our debts, as we also have forgiven our debtors. And do not bring us to the time of trial, but rescue us from the evil one." (MATTHEW 6:7–13)

READER: The word of the Lord.

ALL: Thanks be to God.

PART ONE + ARTICLES 2759–2772 AND 2777–2796 OF THE CATE-CHISM

The gospel

[1] In the gospels, Jesus' disciples knew him to be a man of prayer. Seeing how this touched and affected his life, they asked him to teach them to pray as well, and in response Jesus taught them the fundamental Christian prayer. Luke's gospel provides one version of this, and Matthew's provides another. Our liturgical tradition has retained Matthew's text.

[2] From the earliest years of the Church, a doxology was added to this text, especially for liturgical use. That doxology is used today by Protestants and Catholics alike. We consider the Lord's Prayer to be a summary of the whole gospel.

[3] The Sermon on the Mount in Matthew presents Jesus' teaching on the reign of God, and central to that is this prayer. This prayer, that God's kingdom may come, points to Jesus' whole mission and to all his teachings and actions. The early followers of Jesus prayed this prayer three times daily, making it the backbone of their lives.

[4] It is a community prayer more than a private one. Jesus did not pray to "my Father" but to the God who is Father of all. In the rites of baptism and confirmation, praying the Lord's Prayer signifies initiation into that community of God. Each time any of us prays this we are made new.

[5] In a sense, this is the quintessential prayer of the whole Church. In the Liturgy of the Eucharist, it unites and prepares, occurring after the Eucharistic Prayer and before the reception of communion. The seven petitions of this prayer lay out all our needs before God.

Our Father, who art in Heaven

[6] When we utter the first words of this prayer, we must first shake off our cultural images of what we think a father or mother is like. The very name "Father" is revealed to us by Christ for the very first time in history. Never before had so intimate a divine name been given to us. But, as article 239 of the *Catechism* reminds us, the mystery of God is in his love for us. When we say "father," we do not mean "male head of household."

WE BELIEVE

Praying to the Father should develop the will in us to grow closer to God. It should foster in us a humble and trusting heart. When we pray "who art in heaven," we do not refer to a place but to God's presence in the hearts of the faithful.

---

[7] "God's parental tenderness," the *Catechism* tells us, "can also be expressed by the image of motherhood." God, in fact, transcends all human categories, and our language is impoverished, too poor

to express the mystery of God adequately. God is neither male nor female; God is just God.

[8] We are sons and daughters of God, and we realize this is a privileged calling. Thus, the Lord's Prayer reveals us to ourselves at the same time that it reveals the Father to us. We are adopted by one who loves us eternally, and this creates within us two basic outlooks.

[9] First, we desire to become like God, full of love ourselves, full of compassion and forgiveness. Second, we learn to trust like a child does, trust that God will give his children what they ask in Christ's name.

[10] God is "ours" according to this prayer, not as a possession but as a shared treasure. So, even though there are divisions among Christians, this prayer reunites us and is a summons to all. We never pray this prayer alone but always in the company of the whole Church.

[11] When we pray to God in heaven, we do not mean to suggest a place like downtown or the state of Wisconsin. We refer instead to *a way of being* which is not absent from us but radically present to us. We must eradicate the erroneous ideas of heaven in order to see that the reign of God is among us!

[12] When we who are the members of the Church pray "Our Father who art in heaven," we are professing that we are the people of God, sons and daughters, seeking the reign of God.

Group or personal process

- What image of God comes to mind when you pray? How do you picture God?

- How do you desire to become like God, full of love, forgiveness, and mercy?

- If heaven is not a physical place, what is it? When we say God is "in heaven," where do we mean he is?

PART TWO ✛ **ARTICLES 2803–2827 OF THE** *CATECHISM*

Let us pray

Hallowed be thy name

[13] The first three of the seven petitions draw us toward the glory of God. The final four express our needs. To "hallow" is to make holy and in this prayer it is uttered as an exclamation of a spiritual insight given to us by Christ. Indeed, God's holiness revealed in Christ is the center of the divine mystery.

[14] We share in this universal call to holiness ourselves, washed in the waters of baptism and sealed in the oil of confirmation. The pathway to such holiness is clear but difficult: it is to love and to put aside selfishness and unilateral living. When we proclaim that God's name is holy, we proclaim that love is primary, that we live in the kingdom of justice, and that nothing can stand in the way of our own holiness.

Thy kingdom come

[15] The kingdom of God is already present among us but not yet fully realized. It is among us because of Christ: Emmanuel (God with us); and it is also that condition of the world for which we still hope. It is expressed perfectly in the Eucharist when we are sent forth to love and serve and announce this kingdom. The establishment of this kingdom is the work of the Holy Spirit who completes Christ's work on earth and brings us the fullness of grace.

[16] St. Paul reminds us in his Letter to the Romans, chapter 14, that the kingdom of God is justice, peace, and joy in the Spirit. This is a call to be united with one another in the culture and society in which we live. Hence, we are involved with the growth of the reign of God. Our vocation is to put into action the energies, the grace, and the means we receive to work for justice and peace.

WE BELIEVE

When we pray for God's will to be done, we are uniting ourselves and our will to that of Jesus Christ, his Son. We agree to join in working for the reign of God.

Thy will be done on earth as it is in heaven

[17] According to the Gospel of John, chapter 13, verses 34–35, the will of God was revealed to us in Christ, and this summarizes our entire tradition. "I give you a new commandment," Jesus says, "that you love one another. Just as I have loved you, you also should love one another. By this everyone will know that you are my disciples, if you have love for one another."

[18] It could not be clearer: this is "the mystery of his will," and we

ask insistently for this loving plan to be fully realized on earth as it is within the Triune God in heaven.

[19] We humans drift so easily into unilateral living. We watch a little too much television. We spend a little too much time online. We gradually stop sharing household meals. We work too many hours. Gradually the love with which we began becomes a bit distant, and we drift into living alone together: unilateral living.

[20] Or sometimes the drift is a sudden shift to selfishness: We steal from our workplace. We engage in selfish sexual activity. We hoard our wealth and ignore the poor. We stop being part of parish life. We shift into unilateral living, one-sided, non-communal, and alone.

[21]However, the good news we celebrate is that Christ delivers us from all this by grace and his paschal mystery. By ourselves we are not capable of love, but united with Christ and joined with the Church, we can keep alive the fire of love in our household and community. We become one spirit with Christ. When we pray for God's will to be done on earth as in heaven, we place ourselves at God's disposal and agree to live in the fire of love.

Group or personal process

- What concrete steps can we take to fan the fire of love and avoid the darkness of unilateral living?

- What do you think the new commandment, about which we learned in faith statement #17 above, means for us today? Can we realistically expect love to become the standard by which we live?

We say Amen

Give us this day our daily bread

[22] We know that God provides for us everything that we need, just as any good parent does for his or her child. And yet...Millions starve to death each year and many in the world live in abject poverty. If we pray this sincerely, then these poor belong to us.

[23] We cannot isolate this prayer from the reality that we are called to care for the least of these who are members of God's family. We are called thereby to care for Christ, as we read in Matthew, chapter 25. We cannot escape the call to do justice because it is what God wants. Destitution is not a gospel value, and poverty is a call to share hospitably whatever we have.

[24] But there is another hunger in the human family: the hunger for the bread of life, which is to know and love God. Perhaps we will never feed the hungry until we also feed ourselves with this bread; but unless we feed the hungry, we cannot find God.

WE BELIEVE

In the Lord's Prayer we pray seven petitions. The Amen is our expression of "yes" to them all. "So be it."

---

[25] Hence, we begin to understand the invitation to pray and work, to share Eucharist, and to become what we share. And to do it "this day," not tomorrow or the next day; we must open our hearts and our wallets *today!*

And forgive us our trespasses as we forgive those who trespass against us

[26] This petition is astonishing. Its two aspects swim together and remind us forcefully that we must become forgiving ourselves. We know that God forgives us because that is revealed to us in Christ. But now—and this is daunting for us—we come to understand that God's mercy cannot penetrate our hearts unless we behave like God and forgive those who have harmed us.

[27] Jesus made this particular petition one of the themes in his Sermon on the Mount. And indeed, it is in the depths of our hearts that everything is bound and loosed. We do not have the personal power to forget an offense, but grace empowers us for this loving act.

[28] We are even called to forgive our enemies. Love is stronger than hate. Forgiveness is stronger than offenses. And there is no limit to divine forgiveness: seventy times seven times!

And lead us not into temptation

[29] God actually does not tempt us, and the verb used in the Greek text here suggests another translation might serve better: "do not let us yield to temptation." This is a prayer to the Spirit who is our helper and our strength.

[30] We want our hearts to be made strong. We want to face down that human inclination toward selfishness, sin, and unilateral living and emerge as more loving. This is possible only through prayer, through keeping ourselves attentive to the voice of God echoing in our depths.

But deliver us from evil

[31] This blunt admission of evil and our inclination to submit to it closes our prayer. The prayer that the presider prays at Mass after the Lord's Prayer echoes this and concludes it beautifully:

[32] "Deliver us, Lord, we pray, from every evil, graciously grant peace in our days, that, by the help of your mercy, we may be always free from sin and safe from all distress, as we await the blessed hope and the coming of our Savior, Jesus Christ."

For the kingdom, the power, and the glory are yours, now and forever

[33] As we reach the conclusion of our prayer we pause to offer simple divine praises. We offer an exclamation of our hope and faith; we proclaim our love for God. Indeed, we are intimately connected to God, and our hearts cannot help themselves but to exclaim what we believe. Amen.

Group or personal process

- What other petitions do you bring to God in prayer? How do your own petitions find expression in those found within the Lord's Prayer?

- List again the seven petitions that are found within the Lord's Prayer. For each, tell how you hope to see it come to reality in your life, community, nation, and world.

Prayer

Our Father, who art in heaven, hallowed be thy name; thy kingdom come; thy will be done on earth as it is in heaven. Give us this day our daily bread, and forgive us our trespasses, as we forgive those who trespass against us; and lead us not into temptation, but deliver us from evil. For the kingdom, the power, and the glory are yours, now and forever. Amen.